I0456021

COINCIDENCES

COINCIDENCES

RAQIYA DIAMANTE

Copyright © 2011 by Raqiya Diamante.

Library of Congress Control Number:		2011905290
ISBN:	Hardcover	978-1-4568-9849-6
	Softcover	978-1-4568-9848-9
	Ebook	978-1-4568-9850-2

All rights reserved. No part of this book may be reproduced or transmitted in any form or by any means, electronic or mechanical, including photocopying, recording, or by any information storage and retrieval system, without permission in writing from the copyright owner.

This book was printed in the United States of America.

To order additional copies of this book, contact:
Xlibris Corporation
1-888-795-4274
www.Xlibris.com
Orders@Xlibris.com
94150

Contents

PROLOGUE

In Life we will have many experiences that leave us with thousands of great memories. On the other hand some are bad and we would like to forget. Still there are others that we cannot forget! The author invites you to take a glimpse into her life as she re-lives some very "extraordinary encounters".

Throughout her lifetime she has experienced numerous "other wordly" events. Many of you will 'get it' as you flip through these pages, while others may have some doubts.

Think about this, if there is a "Sea World" and an "Animal World" then there has to be a "Spirit World". Read for yourself about some of her true experiences.

ENJOY!

CHAPTER 1

HIDE-N-SEEK

If memory serves me correctly, I remember I was very small. I had just started school, and only went half of the day. We took a lot of short trips. We have a lot of relatives scattered all around the country and occasionally, whenever my father could fit a trip in, off we'd go if the weather permitted. At times we would find ourselves in Washington or New York. We were from Philadelphia so all of these cities were very accessible, a two-hour drive at most depending on which part of the state we were headed. Very accessible!

Most of the time, we didn't know which way we were going or who we were going to see until we were half way there. This particular day we were headed to New Jersey. Sometimes we would just go to Atlantic City, before the casinos took over, to ride the waves, soak up some rays and swim our hearts out. This day was beautiful, no clouds just real calm and real sunny. When I found out we were going to see my Aunt, Uncle, and their children, I was especially happy! We were all around the same age and we had big fun with my cousins. See we could never leave without playing HIDE N' SEEK. The last time we were here visiting I got caught my brothers and cousins about three times. They always had it in for me. This time I was determined to outsmart them once and for all.

Our people in New Jersey had a large house that sat on a lot of land. Some of it was used for gardening, lots of fruit trees, there was a barn with their farm animals and a small section near the back door of the house for hanging clothes out to dry. Back in the day, people used props (thin wooden "V" shaped sticks on either end) to hold clotheslines up, especially on windy days so the clothes would dry fast and wouldn't drag on the ground. They also had two brick houses at the driveway entrance that sat closer to the highway. We were not familiar with the people who lived there, whenever we saw them outside on the porch we would wave and they would wave back! That was the extent of that.

So after we get there for a while we would sit around, musing ourselves about the latest happenings. We sometimes took the time out to eat some fresh cakes or pies. We knew that sooner or later, we would be gathering various vegetables from the garden. So before it got to that point we left the adults there in the house and we all went outside to play Hide and Seek. We would run to the huge barn so that's where the counting started. Seven, Eight, Nine, Ten . . . . "Ready or not here I come." I had ran the farthest because I wanted to be situated where I could see everybody's hiding place but nobody could see me. I know for a fact that my brothers and cousins all tried to hide somewhere near my aunt's house. I can still remember running and looking back to make sure that nobody followed me.

I was overjoyed to see how everybody was getting caught and tagged, especially my brothers. See I thought about this spot the last time we played this game and it turned out to be the ideal place. All I had to do was crawl under this little brick house, over a few planks and nobody would see me. I think they just gave up, all of a sudden they were calling me and I knew instantly that it would be time to leave soon. I wanted to make them wonder, so I just kept quiet and watched them looking around for me. To me, this was hilarious and I didn't want to laugh too loud. I think it was only fair considering how they had caught me three times in a row the last time we played.

From my hiding spot I could see everybody and I remember thinking we wouldn't have to pick anything out of the garden this time because I could see my aunt and uncle giving my parents bags. You could still see the ears of corn sticking out. They would pass the bags along to my brothers, which meant they must have gone to the garden earlier in the day or the night before. Either way, we didn't have to do it this time. I could see my youngest brother getting into the car, while my oldest was still looking around for me. And there's my cousins coming out of the house. My mother called one last time . . . . okay, okay, "I'm coming", I thought to myself all the while coming out of my hiding place. Then when my father blew the horn to the old Volkswagen and called my name, I knew he meant business, but to tell you the truth I really didn't want to leave. My hiding spot was so nice and cool.

Hurriedly, I've made up my mind to come out and catch up with the rest of the family, when I'm halfway there I noticed one of these wooden planks lying there on the ground. I was wondering to myself where it came from, all of a sudden it took on a life of it's own. I see this prop suspended in the air. It was if some unseen force was standing there holding it just so I could see it, for what seemed like eternity. I remember looking back while I was running and when I was a good distance away it was simply set back down. WOW! Was all I could say because there was nobody there but me and I was in some kind shock at what I had just witnessed! There were no cats or dogs around either. It was not quite dark the sun had not set. I ran as fast as my feet would carry me and I was so out of breath when I got to the car nobody had to tell me twice to get in, I said my "goodbyes" from inside of the car where I felt safe. We could head back across the bridge.

When I felt we had gone far enough, I started babbling, telling my mother about my incident. She had a funny look in her eyes as I was trying to explain the only way I knew how. She just said maybe the wind blew it, but there was barely a breeze blowing even up to that point. I kept talking and she would say things like, "It was just a cat or something", but I knew better. She didn't understand or maybe she did and didn't want to shake me up anymore than I already was. Sticks just don't pick themselves up and move for no reason I thought to myself. I had a hard time going to sleep that night and lay there with my mind racing just thinking about the incident. It just didn't make sense to me . . . .AT ALL. I finally fell asleep beside my mother in her bed. Little did I know that this was only the beginning for me.

CHAPTER 2

VOICES IN THE NIGHT

Sometime went by and now summer was coming to an end and my cousin Stanley came to spend the last three weeks with us. We always had fun whenever we got together as we were around the same age. I was about seven or eight and we had gotten accustomed to having him around.

Sometimes at night we would sit around on the back porch and tell all sorts of jokes, or he would show us some of his magic tricks that were so sad. We tried to outdo each other every night until bedtime. He was an only child and used to tell us how lonely he was so I guess this was one way of entertaining himself and others.

Outside of our backdoor and everybody else on the block for that matter there was a cemetery not ten steps from our back door. A lot of people used it for a shortcut including us when we were going to see someone on the next block over. We often hid our treasures from the day in the backyard and sometimes would check on them at night to make sure they weren't disturbed.

A typical day in our house on the weekends was to get the housework done as fast as you could so we could go out and play with our friends. There were, what seemed like a thousand kids on our block, so there was always something to do. In the short time my cousin became their friend too. They weren't too happy to learn that he would be leaving the next day, back to Chicago. We started school around the same time and he had to get his new school clothes and I'm sure that his mother missed him too.

So after it got dark we were all called inside. We had to take baths and help our cousin finish packing his only suitcase. He would be leaving on an early flight the next morning.

Anyway, we got that out of the way and we all stayed up really late doing silly kids stuff. We did anything to avoid going to sleep that night but one by one we couldn't hold our eyes open so first my brothers went to their room. I helped Stanley get his clothes out of the dryer and soon he went to my brothers' room to conk out too.

I was always the last one to go to bed because I would wait up for my father. He worked a night shift at the post office and when he came home I would stay up just to talk to him. There was nothing I wanted to see on TV and I couldn't engage my brothers in a game or any kind of activity, so it was my time to turn in too.

There was a defect in the floorboard that ran from my brothers' room to my room. It was hard to sidestep so anybody that walked on it you could not mistake where the sound came from. Especially at night the sound was magnified ten times and was impossible to miss.

I got into my bed but for some reason I felt uneasy. I went into my brothers' room and tried to rouse them one last time to play a game or something but they were fast asleep. So I got back into bed trying to doze off with my back to the door. Suddenly I felt a presence got up to look around but there was nobody in my room but me. When I laid back down, suddenly and without warning what sounded like a man's voice whispered in my ear "Yah". The breath was so hot I thought for a minute I was dreaming but I hadn't been asleep at all. I immediately went to my brothers' thinking they were trying to play a trick on me as their room was directly across the hall and that's when I realized that I never even heard the floorboard creak.

To make matters worse they were still asleep because I was prodding them to see what kind of reaction I would get. I was so scared and puzzled I went into my parents' room and stayed right there in the bed beside my mother until my father came home.

I knew I had to tell my father about this when he got home so I waited until I heard him come in and flew down the stairs breathless. I was not sure about his reaction but the first thing on my agenda the next morning was to quiz my brothers. I could tell by their reactions that they thought I had just made the whole thing up and they looked at me kind of dumfounded. They didn't have a clue what I was talking about.

Later we drove Stanley to the airport and that was that but I couldn't stop thinking about that voice and relive that hot breath on my ear many times over. For many years after this incident, I would not turn my back to the door. I was so afraid I would hear that strange voice again and again.

About a week after this incident, I overheard my mother talking to one of our neighbors and she was telling her that sometimes when she went to the basement to do the laundry, which was usually at night, she could hear what sounded like a lot of people whispering. I never questioned her about this. Mabye, I was just too afraid to want to know anything else about this weird house and the things that I experienced. Nothing ever happened to my brothers' that they would admit to but I thought to myself "one day they will see".

Chapter 3

THE BLACK ANGEL

I was going to middle school when I found out that we were moving from the house on Montana Street. I was going to miss everybody on the block terribly. After all, we had all grown up together. I tried to somehow equate my experiences in that house and the cemetery behind it. I was glad that we were moving for that reason. Whoever wanted to buy our house and move in with the spirits or whatever was living there besides my family, they had my blessings! I thought, "Now, I won't have to deal with this strange stuff no more"!

It was early spring we finally settled into our new house. By this time we had new friends and I used to run track after school every day.

This particular day I remember being extremely tired so I decided to lay down to rest before practice. It did not seem to be any longer than fifteen minutes but turned out to be two hours. I looked at the clock and by this time I realized that I had missed my practice, so I just settled back in my cozy bed only—there was a lady sitting on the edge of my bed. She was dressed from another era. She had on a white apron, a white turban and maybe a calico dress and she looked to be not a very nice person. She also looked to be kind of heavy. I only saw her profile but did not recognize her as anyone that I knew dead or alive. I just stared at her for a while longer. A few minutes later I closed my eyes for about 5 seconds and when I opened them again she had disappeared. *She was not transparent in fact, she was very solid.* I was too afraid to touch her or say anything to her seeing how abruptly she had intruded into my life. Who was she? Where did she come from?

After a while about dinnertime I guess while we were eating I asked if we had company around three or four o'clock and was surprised to find out that nobody had been by.

I never mentioned anything about this to my family for fear of ridicule again by my brothers. The next day at track practice, my mind raced back to my afternoon visitor, from the previous day. I chalked it up to one being a weary soul who was on a long, long journey and got lost. Or did she?

A couple of days went by, I tried as hard as I could to block out this experience. Nothing worked! By the end of the week, I felt halfway what I consider normal again. A few more weeks went by but one Sunday night, after I crammed for an upcoming test the next day, I finally dozed off but the dream that I had was disturbing. This same lady that sat on the foot of my bed was "warning" me. This time she identified herself. I'm thinking to myself, "I don't even know you", her exact words were" I am the Black Angel, I'll come to you three times and the third time I will bring you trouble".

I was in somewhat of a daze when I woke up because I usually have a hard time remembering a dream in its entirety unless it was somewhat disturbing, most of the time it's bits and pieces that I can recall.

The next night I had the same dream and this same lady was right there repeating the warning to me again! "This is the second time I am coming to you when I come one more time I will bring you trouble". As I was getting ready for school the next day I remember thinking, "What in the hell did I do to deserve this?" I thought I had left this madness on Montana Street. This was very unnerving to say the least.

I was determined not to let this get the best of me. After all, it was just a dream or was it? The next day while going through my school routine I simply willed myself not to think about this and for the most part just pushed it to the back of my mind. I decided to concentrate hard on my studies and enjoy my friends. I ran track after school and tried to focus on anything to keep from going home and going to sleep. I dreaded it at this point!

I was so exhausted by the time I completed my homework, took my bath, I figured I would just get a good night sleep. Perhaps, she won't come tonight. Up until this point she always had on that same calico dress and white turban just as she had the very first time I encountered her.

This time she had on a white robe and she was speaking an unknown language I didn't understand and finally the last thing she uttered to me was in English when she said "This is my third and last time, I won't come to you anymore".

I was so stunned because this lady knew my name and she did keep her word coming to me three times. Thank God she came only in my dreams as I don't know what I would have done had I come face to face with a character like this.

After this incident, I waited to see what would happen next only I didn't have to wait long.

Chapter 4

Aunt Lola

Everybody has a favorite aunt, uncle, cousin or somebody they hold in high regard. My favorite aunt was named Lola. To me she was beautiful, inside and out. She was stout, wore a blond streak in her hair and always impeccably dressed. Her smile was so bright it would light up a whole room on the gloomiest of days and when she laughed it was infectious. Her teeth were so even and white against that pretty smooth skin, they reminded you of pearls.

She resided in New York with my uncle Robert who was a Master Tailor. It was said that he outfitted some of the most famous musicians of the Harlem era. He would go to their houses, take their measurements and before you knew it he would have finished one suit or whatever he was working on and starting on the next one. He had to work really fast and sometimes these articles of clothing were to be worn that very same evening if not the next day.

My aunt was very fond of children. She had six unsuccessful pregnancies due to the fact that the technology was not as accomplished as it is today. She literally took myself along with my older brother to be her very own. We would spend most summers with her and do all sorts of fun things. I have very fond memories of her. She would have us so spoiled by the end of our visits I can still hear my mother saying it would take her the rest of the year to straighten us out!

There was something mystical about my aunt too although I would not find out exactly what it was until years later when I could understand it better. I could never pinpoint this as a child. Aunt Lola always seemed to have a guest usually women with other children coming or going from this little room. I always wondered what her occupation was. I was told that she gave her patrons the "numbers to play" for a fee. She had great luck betting on the horse races which is still a very big sport up north. Whatever we wanted to do it always seemed like she was up for it. She had more energy than us at times and our summers were well spent with her.

Sometimes we would go to Greenwich Village or Coney Island. The park I remember most is Central park. We always wanted to go there and stay for hours. She always had something new to show us. I think there was an obelisk that is still there if I'm not mistaken.

One day stands out in particular. It was raining earlier in the morning when my aunt asked, "What we wanted to do today?" She promised to take us to the park after she took care of her business. We wanted balloons of course but these were no ordinary balloons. They looked like planets to us I guess because we were so little. So here it was the three of us and we're walking and talking and playing when all of a sudden she stopped and we stopped. She physically separated us. We asked, "Why are we stopping"? She told us to just be quiet and be still, "Let Mr. Simon pass by." We were stunned because we never did see Mr. Simon but she insisted he was right there and apparently we were in the way. Later we found out that her neighbor Mr. Simon had just died a week or so ago and I guess this was one of the ways she gave him his respect as she did know him. We didn't, we couldn't even see him.

It was then that I learned about something that was very common a while back. See, back in the day, whenever people had babies, they sometimes stayed inside at home for about a month. Some of the babies were born with what they call a "veil" over their faces. According to the elders, it is just a very thin piece of skin that falls from the foreheads of the newborns just below their eyes, and it is cut off at birth. It takes about a month for the scar to fully heal. Although no one speaks about this anymore, and I for one have never witnessed this but I'm sure that it still exists with some births.

My brother and I talked about this trip to the park endlessly and then it was dismissed. We just didn't talk about it anymore. We never told our friends either. Although my aunt toyed with us about this she tried to explain it to us . . . we just never understood.

By the way, my uncle also wanted children in the worst kind of way and I remember my mother telling us sometime later that one of the trips he frequently made to one of his customers he had an affair with. Now my aunt being clairvoyant already knew this. One night he was going to check on his customer when my aunt noticed the solemn mood he was in. He made up some story and she made him confess that recently this woman did have a child but the baby died and he was actually on his way to the funeral.

In the meantime, we continued our usual visits if we weren't in school. We made plans to go sometime around Thanksgiving but couldn't get in touch with Uncle Robert for a whole day. Nor did we speak to Aunt Lola, which was really unusual. I knew something was wrong at once because the rhythm was off. The last thing that I expected to hear from my uncle the next day was that my beloved Aunt was dead!

Oh—what a shocker that was. I remember my mother crying hysterically saying over and over again, "Why"? Before I knew it everybody in the house was crying. Through our tears we hastily threw our weekend bags together and headed for New York to see if there was anything we could do for my uncle. He was telling us through sobs, how he had found her lying on the kitchen floor when he came in from work. He was mortified. Aunt Lola was his world in spite of some of the things he had done.

This was my first experience with death. I had never witnessed a grown man crying like a baby. The mood was very somber. Then I remembered my dream about this "Black Angel". Is this the trouble she warned me about? Why did he have to pick my aunt out of all the people in the whole wide world. She was so sweet! I remember being very bitter after that. The following week we went to the funeral. She looked like she was asleep. Since I had never seen a dead person I decided to just walk over to get a closer look. I remember touching her. Her body was ice cold and so stiff. I know because I tried to move her fingers. I just stood there and looked at her for a while. That's how I said my "goodbyes". I personally was all cried out at this point.

We continued to stay in touch with my uncle, but he just got sadder and sadder. We would also visit periodically he was very lonely for a while afterwards. Every time we saw him, I half expected to see my aunt coming out of her little room with her guests following. There was always something missing. I guess it was my aunt's laughter

We didn't see him for about a year but we stayed in touch with phone calls. Five years went by and one day out of the blue my uncle called, he was inviting us up for the weekend to meet his fiancé. It was midday as I recall when we got there.

He said that he had been really sick and this was during the time that they had started this program called "meals on wheels" for the sick and shut in. The nurses at the time made the house calls and deliveries as I recall. He called the agency one day and met his future wife.

So we are all here inside the vestibule and rang the bell. His lady friend answered the door and my whole family went into shock. I just heard one loud "gasp" in unison. We were totally speechless. It was like she had been cloned. I mean this lady was the spitting image of my aunt! I really wanted to hug her and almost asked why she waited so long to come back but I knew better. I know that I saw my aunt lying in a casket. I had even kissed her. She had those same pearly white teeth, the blond streak in her hair and she even had that whimsical laugh and the same complexion. I mean, everything about this lady was my aunt all over again as if she had been reincarnated to comfort my uncle.

As for myself I just kind of stared and watched this lady's every move. My brothers' weren't saying too much either. I was petrified. She was very, very cordial and had almost the same mannerisms. For a minute there I was expecting to hear her say something like my aunt really wasn't dead. We originally planned to spend the weekend but nobody could eat anything and we just couldn't get comfortable.

My mother who never drank anything stronger than water sent my father to the liquor store to get her something strong to drink. Like Jim Beam strong! She was sitting on his lap singing something so loud. I knew it was time to go then. The whole scene was so unreal. We left with a lot of questions going back over the bridge. It was supposed to be a weekend trip but it turned out to be about two-hours. By six o'clock we were pulling back into our driveway and it was still daylight.

I have always heard the elders say that we on this physical plane, all of us have a twin somewhere. Now . . . . I believe it! I saw this with my own eyes only this time I wasn't alone.

Chapter 5

MITTENS

I'll never forget the first time that I saw mittens. My father used to work at the Post Office. I no longer waited up for him but I always heard his door shut when he was leaving the garage to come in the house. We have always had pets since I was a young child. Sometimes it was turtles, rabbits, (1) cat and several dogs. Notice I said 1 cat. That's because my mother was so terrified of cats. Whenever she saw one from our front window she would start hollering at us to make sure they didn't even get in our yard.

Somehow, I think animals innately know whether you like them or not. Since I've gotten older, I realize that some people are allergic to them and others are genuinely just afraid. Why, I don't know. Anyway, when we were getting ready for school the next day, I think I noticed the cat first and went to show my brothers as my mother had already left for work.

He was just sitting there in a corner of the living room trying to get acquainted with his new surroundings I guess. My father told us while we were eating breakfast that when he came home the night before he didn't even notice the cat. When he opened the door he just ran in and since he was too tired to look for him he let him stay. His intentions were to let him back out because he knew that my mother would be afraid.

The next night the same thing happened only this time he just moved right on in so we moved him into the basement. He was unusual to me in that he had such a small but powerful build but his head was the size of a grown man. Our friends would come over and demand that we put the cat in the basement before they would even consider coming inside to visit. Every time I saw mittens he was either coming or going. I mean we kept him fed but there was this window that stayed broken. This was another way for mittens to get out to roam around the neighborhood. He also got into a lot of fights because there was always a scar over his eye or one of his ears and I would always see him licking his wounds. He was a very interesting cat and he had a mind of his own. In fact, most of the time he would leave out with my father when he was going to work, then he would come back scratching on one of the screened windows about one half hour before my father came in and then they would make their entrance together.

This went on for about two years and one day we came home from school to find that there was nobody there. This in it self was unusual because my father would normally be in the den. Most of the time, my father would try to take a nap. He would have to go to work later in the evenings.

After it got dark I was talking with some friends and my brothers when I heard my mother come in. She had this haggard look to her so I knew right away that something was wrong. The news that came with it was a real eye opener. When we finally got rid of our company she sat us down to tell us that she had to take my father to the Veterans Hospital because he had been running a fever but kept putting off the doctors' visit so she had taken him. After that the phone rang and it was the hospital saying that they were going to keep my father because that high fever turned out to be "walking pneumonia".

This was really crushing to hear because I can never remember my father being sick at all. I don't ever recall him even having a cold. This was not the worst of it. The next day they called back and said that they had ran some tests they also found cancer in one of his lungs. I was devastated.

The weird thing to me was this. Mittens didn't come to scratch on the screen door that night or the next for that matter. As a matter of fact as long as my father stayed in the hospital we didn't even see mittens. He didn't even try to come home because I was usually the one who fed him. On the day that my father came back home, we got him together to get out of the car, and then we looked up and see mittens on the doorstep. The whole time my father was home recuperating so was mittens he hardly ever left home. My father went back to work sometime later and mittens resumed his regular schedule. Things were about to get bad, Very bad.

Chapter 6

POPPY

I hardly know where to start when it comes to my father whom I affectionately called "Poppy". To me next to God he was the greatest man in the universe. See, I was a real "Daddy's Girl" My father was my world. I guess I don't have to tell you how close we really were, I worshiped the ground he walked on. Most of time he was very understanding but you didn't want to cross him. His temper was like a volcano when it erupted.

When we started noticing changes in poppy, they were gradual at first. I guess it was the medication he was on because he would be himself one minute and then he would just kind of go into a shell the next and at the same time you didn't know what to expect. For the most part I would say that he was hiding to keep up a good front for us—ALL of us. When we were little he used to tell us all the time that he was invincible, he could do anything and that he was never going to die. I truly believed that after all he was such a very muscular, strong man. We would occasionally ask him how he was doing and he would simply smile and say "alright"! The way that he got around for a sick man you would never know that anything at all was wrong with him. He was still active in church, he still made furniture, he still worked at the post office and still running the family store. I always believed that he would get better as he was also very strong willed.

The hospital visits increased, and so did the medications, there were always more tests. He would drive himself to the hospital for the most part but never said much about the progress. I think he wanted to keep his worsening condition private.

In the meantime, my great, great Grandmother who raised my father and was the only mother that he every really knew without notice had suddenly had a stroke. I can still remember coming home from school one day when the telegram came saying that, "we needed to get there as soon as possible"! We wasted "no time" school, work everything was put on hold. As a matter of fact, that same night we started packing our bags.

It was really dark when we left and I suppose traveling by car is still the norm because there is less traffic in the wee hours and you can make better time getting to your destination and ours was Georgia. The ride started smooth and we were asleep before we knew it.

I remember waking up to hear my father swearing about the car and calling for some help. We managed to get out of the car before it blew up and still salvaged some of our belongings. We had made it to Detroit. My father had to make the necessary arrangements for us with a couple more phone calls. He borrowed my uncle's car so he could see my grandmother before she closed her eyes for good!

By the end of the week he was back looking really sullen. He didn't have to tell me, I already knew that my grandmother was dead. The relatives in Georgia said that she had been asking for him over and over again. We rested up a couple more days with our people there and started out again. There was nothing we could do about the car that blew up we made it by the weekend. We leave in a better car on our way to a funeral.

I was glad to see our people and had not realized just how many people knew my grandmother. It was a massive gathering! It was a rather large church but had no air conditioning. We were smothering and I really don't know whether it was better outside than inside. Anyway, I went right up to view my Grandmother and after that, all the children were in and out until the services were over. We also buried her in the family plot the same day. To tell you the truth I was glad when everything was over as I don't care for funerals to this day and if I could, wouldn't even go to my own.

My father along with his brothers and other relatives were the pallbearers. He looked so haggard and for the first time I noticed how thin he was getting. I also remember his breathing you could hear him all over the church. When we returned from the days events everybody participated in the "Feast." I could hear my mother questioning him but apparently he didn't even realize how loud he was breathing.

When we returned home my father would resume his doctors' visits which by now had to become too frequent. He had shortened his hours at the Post Office and started spending more time at the Veterans Hospital and so were we every single day. Often, it would be well past visitors' hours and we would be getting home well past 11 o'clock at night. The orderlies would just let us stay.

By now, it was like 2 years since my father found out that he had pneumonia and I was really tired of him being stuck up in that hospital. I just wanted to take him home with me to stay for good. That was not to happen! The doctors had to order special tools to cut through his muscles to take out one of his lungs. Up to this point I wholeheartedly thought he was getting better. I had hope again! My mothers' sister had come from Tennessee to help out wherever she could and she had been there for a month. My mother had gotten to the point that she didn't want to be alone my aunt would often would sleep with her at night for that reason. My father when he came home on the weekends would sit in his car for hours on end. Sometimes it seemed like it was 200 degrees and he would be contented just sitting there because he said that he was cold all of the time. His other favorite place was the den and we often heard his labored breathing coming from there.

I started skipping school and would spend most of my days with him. I thought he was going to chastise me as he was such a stickler for education but instead he seemed like he welcomed my visits. I missed him so much. A lot of our relatives in and out of town as well as some of our neighbors started visiting more often now. Mittens would only come home a day ahead of my father and left when he went back to the Veterans Hospital. I often wondered if this cat knew that his condition was getting worse. I realize now that animals have a much keener sense than we humans.

One day when we were talking he told me about a dream he had from the night before. There was this guy whom I'll call Mr. Johnny that was in the next bed over. He was by all accounts a lot worse off than my father. As the dream went he said that this Angel came to my father and told him that he knew how badly he wanted to live. I desparately wanted that for him more than anything in this world. My father said that he spoke to him for a while and the Angel assured him that he could make him whole again. By nature my father was never one to trust anyone too readily so he suggested at the end of the conversation stating, "See about my buddy because he's worse off than me"!

He said that he watched as the Angel walked over to Mr. Johnny and started to touch him at very strategic points. My father described the Angel as being of male gender, very muscular, very tall with a "glowing" white robe. I told him that he was going to be all right too as I gently kissed him I felt a slight chill and really didn't know what to think. I thought to myself maybe it's just the medications. Shortly after that I left so I could sort this revelation out on the bus trip home and I had to come back later with the rest of our family. I thought he was going to tell my mother that I had skipped school but to my surprise, he didn't say anything.

So about two months went by and I tried to visit him more often, and I knew that I could stay out indefinitely and took full advantage of it. I wasn't concerned about my grades anymore. Around this time he also told me that he wouldn't be coming back home. I noticed a distinct sadness in him and the guy that shared his room wasn't there. He told me that they had taken him down for some more tests yesterday. I was kind of surprised because to me he looked like skin and bones and he had tubes running all over the place. My father wasn't like that, he was better off I thought.

In the meantime, while I was watching television here the orderlies came in with Mr. Johnny on a stretcher. For some reason he seemed to have perked up. Now I thought to myself what kind of test could make him feel like that! He looked so alive. Sure wish they would give my father a test like that so he can come back home for good. I would take care of him myself. The next week as it turned out we noticed that my father had a different roommate. After a while my father told us that Mr. Johnny had gone home "cancer free".

Now my hopes were really high. Mr. Johnny came by to see my father a few more times and after that said the doctors had no explanation for his sudden 'healing', he was terminal. So this something that happened had to be nothing short of a "miracle". What else could dissolve this devastating disease, just like that! What about my father? I thought, "He'll be home soon too".

When I got home from school about a week later, I wasn't there five minutes I got the knock on the door and dreaded taking the Telegram from that outstretched hand, that's how I found out about my father's death. I only remember running, crying and screaming at the top of my lungs to my "play mother". I still don't know how I got back home. Mittens never came back home it was like he just disappeared into thin air! My world stopped instantly, I was completely devastated!

Chapter 7

FOOTSTEPS

Have you ever known that certain someone so well that you could recognize their coming in or out of a room by their footsteps alone? Well as a child my brother and I knew instinctively my fathers' steps especially when we were up to no good.

Our house was full of neighbors and the last of the relatives were on their way back home. We had to take my aunt to the train station to and to tell you the truth I didn't want her to go. She had been quite a help to my mother when she really needed her most. I just wanted to be left alone I could hardly eat because I was in such a sad state. You couldn't even mention my father's name without me crying my heart out. My brothers' would get so frustrated and were no consulation whatsoever. I took his death extremely hard and in a way blamed myself. I subconsciously expected him to come through the door any minute and then I would catch myself and snap back to reality.

Things would never be the same at my house ever again. Our home was now nearly completed on the outside but there was still a lot of activity going on. I was so lost and felt like my life should be over too. I gradually got myself together. By now I had finished High school and was pondering my options.

I could not believe that it had been around six months since my fathers' death. Time sure does fly! The same guys who had helped my father build the house were always in and out picking up where they had left off as they also worked at the Post Office. So during the day for the most part we worked on the moldings around the baseboards, windows and doors and other small details. My brothers' had helped to build the house too so it was really special to us. I just kept busy most of the time to try not to think about the recent events.

One day as I was washing the dishes I felt what I thought was a "cold kiss" that lingered on my cheek I thought about my father and the tears would start all over again. This particular day I had rearranged my room took a bath and lay there for hours reading. I had to get up to turn off the light because I didn't have a nightstand. Slowly I drifted off when all of a sudden I hear these footsteps. I lay there in the dark and listened intently. NO—it wasn't one of my brothers getting a snack I got up and turned the light on and the walking stopped. Instantly!

I got back into bed thinking it was my imagination and better yet maybe the guys just forgot to put one of the vents back into the attic portal. I convinced my self that I could be birds or some other small creature bouncing around. I read for another hour or so I guess and felt my nerves had settled enough to turn off the light for a second time and try to get some sleep again. I hoped back into bed and no sooner had I done this when, I heard the footsteps again.

There were two doors in the living room, one led to the patio. I don't recall hearing them open or close. The footsteps were identical to my fathers; but this could not be so. Before his death he told me that he wasn't coming back home anymore. We had even gone to his gravesite to make sure that the headstone was in place. Surely he couldn't have figured out a way to come back home.

I went to my mothers' room to check on her maybe she heard the footsteps too. She was fast asleep so I let her rest. Instead of going back to my own room I walked down the hall and woke up one of my brothers'. We sat up talking and watched television for a while and finally we went to our rooms. I finally drifted off at last to a sound sleep I thought.

About an hour later, I felt a sudden thump at the foot of my bed. I look around but there's nobody there. I was paralyzed with fear. I tried to scream for one of my brothers' but nothing came out and there was that unmistakable sound of my fathers' footsteps. Getting closer it sounded like they were going around in circles, it was pitch black and headed for my room. Just like that the coldest fingers I ever felt ran right through my hair. Without a moments hesitation I jumped up, got the scissors and cut off all of my hair. I was shivering at this point but cleaned up my mess and tried to go to sleep with the lights on this time. It was almost daybreak when I finally dozed off and I guess my mother seeing the light with all of my hair in the trash on her way to work the next morning came in and freaked out. As I explained my latest ordeal she just shook her head on the way out to the car. I really didn't want to bother her with this not at this time but she seemed to have calmed down and never questioned me about it anymore. I was so shaken behind this I kept my hair short for a very long time.

Chapter 8

THE TELEPHONE CALL

It had rained the night before and by ten o'clock the next day it was shaping up to be a pretty nice day. My cousin called and after a long conversation we decided to hang out later at the ballpark to see what we could get into. I needed to get back to the land of the living it was time for a change. It has been about eight months now of brooding and today I would try to get out and have some fun. There was so much housework to do because I wanted to make sure the guys were finished with the molding on the inside so I could get rid of that mess for good.

First I fixed breakfast for my brothers' and myself and since this was a typical Saturday, there was no need to rush. After we ate I went to my closet to see what I wanted to wear. My mother had gotten out earlier to visit some of our relatives in New Jersey. I had gone next door to catch up on the latest gossip and circling the block I ran into my best friend. We wound up at the corner store loaded up on our goodies for the game she came back home with me and stayed a while.

Before I realized it we were talking so much it was almost twelve thirty and she had work to do as well. While she was leaving, my brothers' came back home to pick up their baseball gear. It was long enough for me to let them know that I had to finish cleaning and with that I started locking all the windows and doors.

This for me was a common practice because my brothers' were always coming and going with their friends. Sometimes they would ring the bell but mostly they would just barge in even though they had keys. I didn't want to get caught off guard. I tried not to dwell on my father so just stayed busy most of the time. After dusting all that was left was vacuuming I would be finished for the day. It didn't take as long as I thought and I realized at this point that I needed a shower.

So I start putting my cleaning supplies back in place and got my clothes together while running a hot shower. The den where my father spent a lot of time in his latter days was right down the hall next to the bathroom. I started ironing a pair of jeans when the telephone started ringing. There was nothing like a cell phone back in the day and we didn't know anything about an answering machine either. So at first I just ignored it, I thought to myself, "If it was something important the person would call back". Right now I had one thing on my mind, *I wanted to go to the game.* Ring, Ring, Ring, it was incessant and it must have rang about 30 times. I'm there with this towel wrapped around me ironing away and it just keeps on ringing. In that instant I thought about my mother who had gone out earlier something could have happened to her so I decided to go ahead and answer it. I had to turn the water off first, only by the time I reached the doorway to the den and started toward the phone I heard what sounded like someone pick up the phone and lay it down softly on top of the television. I was speechless! I was expecting to hear someone on my end say "hello." I went through the house to see what was going on but there was nobody there. I started shaking and somehow managed to put the phone back on the hook. I pulled my towel around my body a little tighter and ran as fast as I could to my neighbor who was also my "play mother". I was breathless and wound up taking my shower at her house while telling her the story of my latest encounter. She was a real comedian and made light of the fact saying, "Maybe the phone rang so hard it jumped off the hook". I think she was just trying to make me feel better. I found some jeans and old "T" shirt and that's where I stayed until I saw some form of physical life came back to my own home. I'm sure that my neighbors thought I had lost my mind completely but I didn't have time to think about that.

By this time the game is over and everybody's asking me what happened and why I didn't show up! We checked all the windows and doors and they were still locked! No! This is impossible, things like this just don't happen. I could not understand why none of this stuff ever happened to my brothers. All of this was very unnerving to say the least and I made it my business not to be alone for a long time.

Chapter 9

Strange Argument

Sometime went by and I eventually got married and had to little sons five years apart. They truly were the joy of my life. When I think back now I realize that I was too young to be married and probably married for all the wrong reasons. I should have pursued my dream of becoming a hair designer but this is how it wound up. My children were a great source of comfort to me. This is not to say that my incidents had stopped by no means.

When my eldest was about nine months old I had fed him and laid him down for a nap. We had been out earlier getting immunizations and we were exhausted. I knew that he would probably sleep a little longer. I can still remember sitting down with my sandwich to watch the news. At first I didn't notice the laughter I thought it was part of the commercial or something like that. It gradually got louder so I turned the sound down to really listen. It had only been about fifteen minutes and I knew that my son was fast asleep. I soon realized that these sounds were not coming from the outside so I peeked into his room and there he is sitting up laughing his heart out. I looked around and didn't see anything unusual so I asked him what was so funny? He made a face and said, "mama him funny". Instantly I felt a chill although, it was not cold inside or outside for that matter. When we are leaving out he turned and was waving at someone or something. I couldn't get out of the room fast enough. I brought him into the living room with me so I could finish my sandwich. He was asleep again within a half hour. I laid him down on the couch to finish out his nap.

Later when my husband came home I mentioned this to him, he just shrugged it off. Earlier in the week I had started sorting out my family pictures and it occurred to me that I should show my son a picture of his grandfather. I gave him a bath and watched him waddle over to the pile of pictures. Almost immediately he grabbed my fathers' picture like he knew him personally yet my father had died three years before he was born. He ran over to me repeating, "Him funny". So I guess that was my answer as to who was in the room with him that afternoon!

When my second son came along my marriage was in trouble and we started having all kinds of problems. To make a long story short it was coming apart from all seams and I eventually filed for divorce. Toward the end we had been arguing a whole lot about everything and nothing. One of our last arguments was over the bikes that I insisted would stay in the backroom with the toys if we were not using them. When I got in one day and found all these greasy dirty parts all over my freshly cleaned rugs I was highly upset. I think sometimes my husband did things to aggravate me. He knew how to press my buttons. That's what started the argument but right in the middle of it, what looked like a rather large black furry basketball, rolled in slow motion right in between us. Needless to say that we stopped arguing immediately and spent about 45 minutes trying to find out what it was and where it went. We never found it. Years later we were still very good friends and occasionally this subject would come up from time to time.

Chapter 10

ATRAL TRAVELING

The first snow had fallen and by now we had moved in with my mother. Now we had the task of unpacking. My sons were excited about staying at their Grandmothers' house. They would be a lot of company for her because she wasn't going out as much as she used to these days. My brothers' would be out later with their families to shovel the snow and my boys would probably pitch in. Besides, they wouldn't want to miss out on a good snowball fight!

One of my mothers' oldest and dearest friends Ms. Lillian, had been on my mind a lot lately. I had known her since I was a child myself. She was the one that gave us neighborhood kids a "Back to School" party every year. I briefly spoke about her with my mother and decided to pay her a visit in a couple of days. If I stopped unpacking now I wouldn't get anything else done. So as I watched my sons playing from the window I busied myself with sorting their clothes in the dressers.

It would be time for me to go to work before I knew it. I had taken a job at a nursing home about ten miles away. The graveyard shift wasn't so bad after three o'clock a.m. time went by pretty fast. While changing shifts, I overheard some of the nurses talking about the five more inches we got overnight. They were telling all of us to be careful because it was very icy. What normally took about twenty minutes to get home turned out to be an hour or more. God! The roads were so icy and snow was piled high as far as you could see. I called my mother to check up on my boys but they had already left for school. When I finally got home I was so exhausted it was all that I could do to jump in the tub. While sipping some tea I heard my mother making her way down the hall. She peeped in my room long enough to tell me that, "They found Ms. Lillian dead this morning and it was said that she had froze to death". This was hard to imagine because this was a tight knit neighborhood and anybody would have gotten her some fuel if they knew she needed it. She could have spent the night at our house for that matter! I just didn't understand how this could have happened.

At once, I looked out the window toward her house. I stood there reminiscing and regretting that I had not gone to visit her a couple of days earlier. I was really mad at my self. I went over to her house partly to be nosy and to see if there was anything I could do as I really didn't know her relatives.

When I finally fell asleep I laid down in the den around one o'clock. Locking the door behind me it was extremely cozy lying in there and I could see why my father liked it so much. I don't know how long I had been asleep when this angel appeared and called me by name. She said to me point blank, "You have a strong desire to travel all over the world don't you"? "Yes", I answered. "Are you ready"? Again, I answered yes! Off we went—She pointed out The Eiffel Tower, Paris, Rome, Germany and Egypt (just to name a few) faster than the speed of light. I wondered how she knew about my hearts desire to travel like this, I never revealed this to anyone. I remember feeling weightless and time—What time???? It happened so fast. I was in a very lofty place and the angel pointed out a lot of things to me all at once. I lost count of the stars as we went through many galaxies to go on this trip.

I remember coming back with this angel right through the wall. Things happened so fast I didn't have time to be shocked. I actually saw myself lying there on the couch in a deep sleep. The angel turned to me and said, "See that's your body why don't you go over and wake yourself up?" I'm hovering over myself not two steps away from the couch when I hear "BOOM, BOOM, BOOM" on the door. It's my noisy youngest son, "I'm starving". Let him tell it he was always starving. I remember pinching my self before I open the door. I smothered him and my oldest son with kisses. I had never been happier to see them in my life. While cooking dinner I couldn't help turning this over and over in my mind. It felt like every fiber in my being had just been turned inside out! We ate, did homework and then my boys played outside for a while.

I just had to tell somebody about this experience. This was Major! I went over to my "play mothers" house where my story unraveled. She usually made light of everything I believe to put my mind at ease. After all she had known me since I was a child, she never once called me "crazy" and she could keep secrets. I knew she would understand no matter what. She had this funny look in her eyes and before I left she said, "You know if you had touched yourself, you probably would not have woke up". I thought about that for a while and I wondered had she had a similar experience? In the meantime, I kept pinching myself and hugging her to reassure myself that I was still on a physical plane.

A few weeks passed when a co-worker of mine rode with me to pick up some pizzas. I was still reeling from my last encounter when I stumbled upon this station. Here it's this late night host giving a lecture on (of all things) "astral traveling". I listened intently and realized that this must be just what I experienced. There was no other explanation. I read some of the books he suggested because I had to have a logical explanation. Since then I've learned that this is possible if one is in a trance and of course there are other factors to consider.

Out of all my travels I must say that this was the ultimate trip for me I didn't need a passport and it didn't cost a dime. Even now when I sit down to watch the educational channels I think about this trip. Certain things about Egypt and other parts of the world are very familiar to me because I was there in another dimension. Another place in time!

CHAPTER 11

THE BICYCLE

My sons were really growing up fast and they were like night and day! Our neighborhood was full of children. My oldest son is like around nine years old now. He is a very sensible and laid back kind of fellow. He had a new companion these days. A pit bull that I was not very fond of. See these dogs have a terrible reputation. It was actually his classmate Matthew's dog but he would never go to his home, which was only on the next block. I mean he would come with his owner hang out for a while sometimes and just stay. We just got used to him being on the doorstep waiting for my son. Wherever my son went this dog was never too far behind.

On the other hand my youngest son was around four now and a real busy body. He was 110% boy and always getting into stuff. It was nothing for him to come in with a brand new scar everyday. When asked how he got some of these nicks and scrapes he couldn't begin to tell you. He was just a tough character and real piece-of-work! For him to have made it to adulthood was a minor miracle.

For the longest my youngest wanted his very own bike. I was contented with his sharing his brothers' bike for the simple reason he was so reckless. Anyway, the Christmas season was fast approaching. Like most procrastinators I hadn't even thought about shopping. I knew that my own mother and my "play mother" would be satisfied with just about anything. I would have to force myself to start somewhere so why not start with the clothes first then the toys.

I got up early the next morning to meet their father. We were going to Delaware where there are no taxes on merchandise and also a few military bases along the way. Against my wishes it was his decision to get this bicycle with the understanding that our purchase would be out two weeks before Christmas. I never entertained the thought of buying this bicycle do to the fact that I knew how wild my son was. My argument was he simply was not mature enough for any kind of bicycle. When he was five or six I could see it, in the meantime he would just have to be contented to share his brothers' bike.

I went to work that night feeling half way satisfied mainly because the majority of my shopping was over. The only ones left were my brothers', nieces and nephews. I actually had off the next couple of days as some of us had worked doubles earlier in the week due to co-workers illnesses. I was looking forward to spending two whole days with my boys. We would definitely spend one of those days at the Planetarium and check out the Dinosaurs too. We did that!

The next day it was sleeting when we got up and we just hung out at home. We went out for some ice cream at this dairy but not too far. Before I went to sleep, I could still hear my sons' up, chit chatting with my mother. In this dream of one of my neighbors came running over to my house screaming, "Your son just got hit on that bike"! As the dream progressed there's my oldest son by my side. My tears flowed like a river. My son had made his transition and there he was lying in this casket. I kept blaming myself because I didn't want him to have this bicycle in the first place. My oldest son was steady trying to comfort me as he tugged on my arm saying, "You still have me"! When I woke up my eyes were still kind of moist. I immediately went to my boys' room. I felt better momentarily.

When I relayed this to their father he insisted it was only a dream but I knew better. This dream was like the worst scene in a bad, bad movie and was replayed three times night after night. No! This by no means was NOT A ORDINARY dream and I took it as a warning!

I continued shopping every chance I got picking up a few presents a little here and there. Before I knew it I was finished and for reasons I can't explain I had bought a wagon. When I met up with their father a few weeks later, it was to get all of my son's stuff out of layaway. I was surprised to find the traffic was so light. This could only mean one thing. The stores would be packed. I was right! When we get there it's wall-to-wall people and some had just started their shopping. We had to maneuver our way through the crowd as if we were going through a maze all the way to the pick up window. Finally, it's our turn and I hand the cashier the ticket for our merchandise. I expected the transaction to be no longer than a half hour but everything was right there in front of us in about 20 minutes. We check the carts to make sure we had everything. It was then that their father noticed that the bicycle wasn't there. We stood off to the side so others could get their orders. I assumed that it would take a few more minutes and it was understandable as we had three carts of goods. The cashier directed some of her co-workers to another department and when they came back about 15 minutes later they were empty handed. The cashier apologized for our inconvenience stating, "We could not find your order anywhere". She offered to let us look but we couldn't find it either. I still don't know why they couldn't find it and I didn't ask. We paid for everything else and left.

Christmas Eve I decided to wrap the wagon and put it under the tree still in the box. When I was taking pictures I watched as my sons' eyes light up with joy as they moved from one present to another making a big mess. To my surprise when he got to the box and found out it was a wagon he showed no signs of disappointment. I still have this picture somewhere. I was relieved and to me it seemed like he had more fun with that little red wagon because he hardly bothered his brother about his bicycle. Their buddies thought the wagon was pretty cool too. Matter of fact I noticed that some of the children from the neighborhood had started to get wagons too later in the upcoming year either for birthdays or some other occasion.

The summer was coming pretty fast and so was the end of another school year. I had just pulled into the driveway when one of my neighbors stopped to tell me that, "Matthew just got hit on his bike". When I got around the corner they had already put him in the ambulance his father rode with him. I went over to his mother who was mortified. She was hysterical beyond words. Myself along with some other nosy neighbors tried to help her get herself together. I couldn't help but remember that dream I had shortly before the holidays. I thought to myself, "That could have been me". I was very grateful that I did not get that bike for my own son. Little Matthew was also "deaf". While playing in front of his house this car tore down the street hitting him and left him with a lot of internal injuries and fractures. Needless to say that he spent a lot of time in the hospital but by the end of summer he was well enough to go back to school. And his dog still sat on our doorstep waiting for my son. To this day I still think my dream was a premonition.

My boys' played with Matthew everyday. My youngest son eventually did get a bicycle for his sixth birthday. He rode it for two weeks when one of my neighbors came to tell me that he was watching him playing outside and he almost got hit. I took the bike apart and left it at my mothers' house for one of my nieces or nephews. It stayed there and we relocated some time later.

Chapter 12

Unseen Hands

I always wanted to live in Georgia, and when I found out that I had gotten this job at one of the hospitals there, I jumped at the chance to move. There were over three thousand gangs in Philadelphia when I decided to leave. I refused to let my boys get mixed up in stuff like that. Life is too short as it is. I was also tired of fighting with those long, cold, snowy winters among other things. When we left Philadelphia we relocated to the suburbs of Atlanta where my uncle lived. We had a lot relatives there too some we knew and some we didn't. My mother really didn't want us to go but she understood. Besides my brothers and their children would be checking on her all of the time. I was hoping that they would want to relocate too. I had sold some of my furniture to cut down on the load. I promised my mother my boys would visit often.

We stayed with my uncle for a couple of weeks while setting up our new place. My aunt had some rental property and this duplex was the ideal spot for us. In the meantime, there was also another family that would be moving right next door to us. I found them to be rather peculiar. After careful observation in a short time I realized that they would be nothing but trouble so we kept our distance, nothing more than a casual "Hi and Bye.

Although my boys missed their friends they had so many cousins and did fit in to an extent. Against my wishes I allowed my son to join "Job Corps" . . . This was quite a change from "The city of "Brotherly Love".

This place was not what they were used to at all because at home there was always something going on but here it was a bit slow and laid back. I liked it though and I liked my job too it was minutes from my house. I got to know quite a few of my neighbors as well.

One day while I was at work one of my co-workers and elderly lady flew into my office as she breathlessly blurted out, "Your house is on fire". At first I panicked because my youngest son who was now a freshman in High School was there alone. I knew we had breakfast together lunch was laid out so he didn't have a reason to cook. Besides I would be home before he needed to eat again. Over the weekend he had come down with a bad case of bronchitis. The medication that the doctor prescribed was so strong, it would have him so groggy and he would go to sleep almost immediately. He would have to take at least four dozes a day. By Wednesday he would be better and we could cut it down on the dosages to twice a day and hopefully he could go back in school.

The hospital where I worked was about five blocks away but seemed a lot further for some reason. With each passing minute, I prayed to God, "Please take care of my son let him be alright". When I got there it was mass chaos with the fire trucks all over the place ambulances, the works. I immediately asked about my son. "Where is my son", I demanded. I didn't care what I lost as long as my son was all right so was I. To me, nothing else mattered, I could always replace the material things. My uncle was right there standing outside of my house and as I approached him my son comes out of one of the neighbors house across the street. I cannot begin to tell you what a relief that was. I couldn't stop holding and kissing him for about ten minutes. I was so happy that my child got out before the fire got too bad. He was my biggest concern.

While I was standing there with my uncle and son, the "Fire Marshall" came up to us, that's when I was informed that, "Had this fire burnt about fifteen more minutes the whole place would have exploded due to all the different gases that had formed". I didn't let my son out of my sight instead I kept hugging him and as I looked at some of the debris that now cluttered the lawn on the neighbors side I couldn't help but think how lucky we were. There was a bookcase out there with charred books but I really didn't think too much of it at the time.

When I asked my son what had happened he shrugged his shoulders and said, "After he took his medication he started dozing off and then he felt something that was like a "Big Hand" that shook him. He saw the smoke and while he was running to the neighbors across the street he heard this loud noise when he looked back the window had exploded and that's when they called the fire department". Again I thanked God for saving my child.

Upon closer inspection I go through my house to see if I could salvage anything. I was glad that I had very little smoke damage to my furniture and walls. The smell lingered in the air and I was grateful for firewalls. Everything else on my side was fine. About the same time, those peculiar neighbors' that lived next door, showed up in my driveway they came out of nowhere trying to explain to anyone who would listen how this happened and how sorry they were. It seems like this little boy who lived directly behind us had become acquainted with her children. She claimed he was responsible for setting the fire! That's what the newspaper said too. I wondered why she and her children didn't smell of smoke or have any soot on themselves. Like where were they when all this damage was caused on their side? I also wondered why she would allow him in her house knowing that he should be in school but really didn't have time to dwell on that. Many mornings when I was leaving for work, I would notice him walking away from the bus stop and smoking cigarettes. He couldn't have been over ten or twelve years old at the most.

I gathered some clothes to spend the night with my uncle. Saturday when I went to pick up my son from the "Job Corp" I told him about the incident and we decided to go next door to look at the damages. Apparently it was a very intense fire and from the looks of things nothing could be saved. It had blown out the front window and everywhere we looked everything it was black and burnt. This was a very intense fire, even the doorknob had melted! We left for fear that we would fall through the floor or something.

When we got back outside, I could see that a collection of "star wars" was scattered in front of the burnt bookcase. I get a little closer and see that quite a few more books are related to "witchcraft" it sent a chill through me. I told my son, "I knew there was something strange about these people". This couple's version of events just didn't add up but still I was grateful my son was alive as it could have been a lot worse.

Monday was the start of a new week. When I got to work my nosy co-workers asked about the fire. They inquired about the little boy who supposedly set the fire. I didn't know anything about him or his family except he had little or no supervision. I really didn't know what he look like until the day of the fire.

My youngest son always had football practice after school and he would usually be home by five thirty maybe six at the latest. Most of the time I had already cooked so he could eat when he came in. The food would still be in the oven to keep warm. I did this everyday because he was always starving! Now lately when I lay down at night, I would get up periodically to check on my son and look around my house to make sure things were all right. This little boy (firebug) was still wandering around the neighborhood but if I caught him around my house I was calling 911. I did a lot of cat napping and really didn't sleep well at all. I finally did buy a sleep aid to rest better. It was unusually warm for January but then again this is the south and this was a very mild winter. I felt drained after taking the pill and a hot bath I could hardly keep my eyes open. The pill worked really fast. I could still hear the news and as I drifted off I felt the covers being pulled up to my chest and someone or something with caring hands patting me as if to say things will be all right. I sat straight up and looked around, trying to collect my thoughts I called out to ask my son why he had put these covers on me because it was so hot. At the same time I hear this "thump" that's him coming through the front door with his football gear, and school bag on the floor. I tried to collect my thoughts while he's approaching my room he has nothing in his hands. I asked him, "Why had he put these covers on me"? I heard him wash his hands and get his plate. When he came back he looked at me with his mouth full and said, "I just got here"! I could see that he had barely touched his plate. This was too much for me to comprehend right now.

I talked to him while he finished and we ate some dessert together. I went to sleep after that and surprisingly I slept all night. I felt kind of groggy the next day but that didn't stop me from getting to my aunt's house. I never said anything to my son about this but I sure broke my neck to tell my aunt about it.

By the way, those peculiar neighbors that lived on the opposite side of me moved to another house and started another fire almost immediately. I don't know what happened to them and I never heard from them again.

Chapter 13

Torn Soul

It had been a few years since I saw my mother. My youngest son had spent some time with her the previous summer. She had been down quite a few times to spend some time with us as well and the last time it was for my youngest sons' graduation. I stayed in touch with her by calling and having many long conversations on the weekends. I had talked her into going on a cruise. I had told her about my last trip to the islands and all the fun she could have. Now with my vacation coming up we could spend it together. This would be her first so I didn't want anything to go wrong.

In the meantime, I had been trying to get my youngest brother to move south. We had talked about it for over three years now and finally he was coming in a few months to live. We were very excited about this. He didn't have any children either so I was certain he would like it as much as I did. I was in a good place in my life. He could stay with me until he got on his feet. My oldest son is now cutting everybody's hair. He has turned into a pretty good Barber. My youngest has gone onto take courses in heating and air conditioning.

I had just gotten in from work one day when I got a call from one of my childhood friends. She was practically screaming and talking so fast I had to calm her down to understand what she was saying. I kept repeating, "What happened"? The last person I expected to hear about was my youngest brother I wasn't even prepared for what had happened. At first I thought she said that he had been shot but it was the other way around. He had been taken into custody and he was hurt real bad. It was really self-defense but he got the charge. I thought about this as I sat down in a daze. I was glad to hear that he would be all right but couldn't imagine how this could have happened.

My brother was not one to look for trouble. Honestly, he would try to sidestep it at all costs. When my childhood friend got there on the scene after everything happened she called me. When I called my mothers' house, it was actually my sister-in-law that I spoke with. My mother was really "shook up" about this. This was so out of character for my brother. He never bothered anybody. Later, I called my other brothers' to see why they hadn't called to tell me. Apparently, since they weren't living in the neighborhood any more one of the neighbors had called them and they were just leaving the police station. Seems like some punks who didn't even know my brother had jumped him while he was working on one of his cars.

It was well after twelve p.m., my nerves were so unsettled as I lay there tossing and thinking about this practically all night. None of this made any sense and it seemed like it was so uncalled for. Within a couple of weeks I flew back home. There wasn't a whole hell of a lot that I could do but I knew that I could do something. We put our money together and got a lawyer. I saw my youngest brother while I was there which was really heart breaking he was really pitiful. I promised that I'd be back to see him as soon as I could. When I got back I gave my sons' all the details. They couldn't believe their favorite uncle was sitting in jail for anything after he spent so much time telling them not to do this and that. They gave me some money to put on his books and I made sure that he got it.

A couple of days go by and while I'm talking to my oldest brother right in the middle of the conversation he got a phone call. Now my first thought was of my youngest brother. When he called back he said it was about my mother—seems like she had a "nervous breakdown". He had saw her earlier in the day and said she seemed fine. "O Wow"! This was not good and most likely it had to do with the recent shooting incident involving my brother. They would be keeping her in the hospital for a few days.

Instead of her coming back home to our family home they were sending her to an assisted living home I found out later on. She could have easily stayed with any one of us but they said she couldn't be left alone. As soon as I get there, I didn't stop until I took her to our family home and tried to make her comfortable. I took her to a lot of doctor's appointments and that's when I found out that she had "Dementia". Before any of this happened I noticed that whenever we talked she forgot a lot of things but I attributed that to part of aging. It's truly amazing how fast this disease progresses.

A few years earlier my "play mother" who went downtown at least three times a week, one day couldn't find her way back home. Now I would catch my own mother staring into space on several occasions. She was also developing "Alzheimer's at a rapid pace. To make bad matters worse this disease was irreversible. This is a lot on my plate all at once but as I'm digesting all this information it was decided that she would come to stay with me. Something had to be done RIGHT NOW! She didn't want to come at first but after talking to her sisters' she calmed down and soon we were back in Atlanta. Things were never the same for her. My sons' did what they could but everybody was working and it was really difficult. A nurse started coming by everyday but it seemed to me like it wasn't doing too much good. I mean like my mother she wouldn't even know who I was sometimes.

Around the same time my oldest son started complaining about his stomach. At first I thought it was a hernia. He went to the doctor and found out otherwise. I suggested we go together to get a second opinion. When I found out it was cancer, I was mortified. He was still a very young handsome man. "How did he get this"? I had a million questions for the doctors' but none of what they said really satisfied me. They determined he had "Hodgkin Lymphoma" and it was spreading. At first I had no idea what this was and did some research on it. There were two tumors the size of basketballs but you would never know it if you looked at him unless he told you himself that he was sick. This was like in March and I went into overtime supporting my son all the way. The doctors' assured us that he had a good chance of beating this disease because of his youth. The right treatments would have to be very aggressive to be affective.

I constantly sent many a prayer up to the Creator, "Please heal my son". If I could I would have traded places with him as he had so much to live for. I knew one day he would want to have a family as he loved children and I looked forward to having some grandchildren to spoil. However, my youngest son would soon take care of that. He would soon let us know that his long girlfriend had went to the doctors and found out she was pregnant.

As the disease progressed he seemed like he was responding well to the treatments. One day he took a turn for the worse his voice was so little and you had to listen closely to hear what he was saying. I prayed so much for him I didn't have time to pray for myself.

Thanksgiving was coming and I made a great dinner with all his favorites. I made a lot of sweet potato pies just for him. He barely touched it saying he would eat later but he never did. I would sit up with him at night until I got tired but I couldn't really sleep. I guess being up with him all hours of the night, finally took its toll on me. I would tip toe into his room watching over him constantly as he was unable to work by now and was staying with me.

The day before he made his transition a friend of the family came over he rode with him to see a few people as he was still kind of active he wanted to check to see how his buddy was coming along with his car. When he asked for some chicken noodle soup I ran to the store to get a few cans because he was not eating very well these days. He had been sleeping a lot lately and when I got back from the store I think the sound of the door shutting woke him up. He asked me if I would take him somewhere where there were a lot of children. I told him as soon as he got a little stronger I would. When I asked him why? He said that, "These children kept coming to play with me every time I close my eyes". I felt a little unnerved by his answer as I looked around the empty room but tried to reassure him that it was only his angels. I knew he always loved children and I wanted to take him to a playground as soon as it warmed up a bit.

I headed for the kitchen and warmed up the soup hoping that he would eat at least one can. He took a few bites said the soup was good but, "It's too heavy for my body". I should have known that there was something wrong. I stayed really close to him these days when I wasn't working. My youngest son had been spending all day everyday with him. He even quit his job. There was no need to go back to the hospital because they had done all they could. He didn't want to go back either he just wanted to be around family mainly with no more poking and probing from the doctors. Nobody wants to see their child go through something like this you feel so helpless. I often asked him how he felt but he never complained.

Now when I laid down that night I had a dream similar to his. Toward the end as I watched the children laughing and playing a game of tag when this little chunky guy ran up an hit me on the arm saying, "Your it"! I looked behind him there was a man standing there in this glistening white robe it was so bright in this place it looked like there were many suns. Right after that I woke up and looked at the clock it was not quite five thirty a.m. I shut off the alarm and went straight into my son's room to check on him.

He wasn't there so I see a light under the door of the bathroom and heard him in the shower. When he came out we talked while I got ready for work. He seemed like his old self laughing and talking as I relayed my dream to him. He didn't have too much to say but seemed like he wanted me to hurry up. As I kissed him it seemed like the room was filled with all these hushed voices yet, I knew that the television wasn't on. I didn't have time to investigate, just finished my coffee and left. He hugged me real hard as if to say "goodbye". I knew that my youngest son who lived about a mile from me now would be there around seven after he dropped his girlfriend off at her job. I would be home at lunchtime to check up on him. This was two weeks before Christmas.

Before I got to work that morning, I heard a little still small voice say, "He won't be there when you get back". Later when I relayed this to some close friends someone told me that I should have turned around right then and there. I remember thinking, "Of course my youngest son would be out with him" as he did any and everything he could to make him happy. By seven thirty I got a call from him stating that my son "was dead". This can't be, I was just talking to him while he laid in my bed catching up on the news. A sharp pain pierced my heart and then my stomach as if I were in labor. I thought I was going to lose my mind. My supervisor ran over to me to find out what happened as she said I screamed but I don't remember this. She drove me home and tried to calm me down. I dreaded every mile the closer we got. When I saw him laying on the bathroom floor it felt like my soul was being torn right of my being as I had a hard time seeing my oldest like this and the tears really flowed. I was pissed to find him lying there like an animal but later I understood why he had gotten out of bed. You are just not supposed to bury your children.

When my youngest son found his brother he said he freaked out too. First he punched a hole in one of my walls. He had thrown himself across his chest and said he sounded like he was "sizzling". He told me that he had a slight smile on his face and his hand was outstretched as if he was about to shake someone's hand. As I looked down at my son I took some comfort in this thinking maybe the "Creator heard my prayers after all as he didn't have a chance to really suffer. Together we put him back in my bed where I washed him again and noticed small unusual welts forming on his skin. Later I was told that this devastating disease was about to eat right through his bones. As I held him I thanked the "Creator again for sparring him that pain. The last time that he was in the hospital he had told us how the lady in the room next to him screamed night and day because she was in so much pain. Maybe that' s why he was rushing me out the door earlier. I do think he knew that his time here on this plateau was near the end I know if I had to watch him take his last breath I would be in an asylum right now. Somehow I blamed myself thinking if I had been there he would still be alive. In reality there was nothing I could do and I've learned to accept this.

I will always miss my son immensely. I feel to this day as we were very close. Not a day goes by that I don't think of him. The peculiar thing is whenever there is a life-changing event that's going to affect me he still comes to me in my dreams. Many days I have come home and felt a presence that I could never touch but I knew that something was there. I can't help but think that this is one of the ways whenever one crosses over to the other side they use this means to stay in touch with us as *the living* are never alone.

He's always in this super bright place like in a lovely garden and that is a great comfort to me. He always looks like he is in great health and it is peaceful, very peaceful no suffering. I can't help but think what is it really like on the "other side" as I know my time is coming too I sure hope he is there. I felt so empty deep down inside where nobody could see I no doubt had lost a large piece of me forever. It felt like the earth was closing in on me because nothing had touched my heart like this before. This was a bitter pill to swallow and I knew that it would take some time for me to get a grip. We never celebrated Christmas anymore after this.

Chapter 14

Fingerprints

Every year we have a family picnic. We had missed out the last two years so we had to go to this one to keep the static down from family members. I couldn't believe four years had passed by so quickly since my son made his transition. My youngest son dropped by often usually to tackle my "leftovers" for his lunch.

By now, I had two grandchildren and they kept me laughing all of the time. Even though my oldest son was deceased and had no children of his own, my grandson looked exactly like him. A lot of friends and relatives noticed this too and would often make comments.

Well the picnic would be in a couple of weeks so I started with the cakes and froze them. Next the pies that everybody was addicted especially my sons then I would be finished. On the day of the picnic there was a lot of excitement and lots of calls. We were looking forward to seeing the rest of the family and catching up on the news. After we got the cars and the children situated the last thing to go into my car would be the cakes and pies. I purposely put two aside and left them on the counter to surprise my son later.

We had a great time seeing some of our older relatives and meeting the newest little cousins. I couldn't wait to show off my "gems" my grandchildren! We stayed until the clouds rolled in and left around seven o'clock. When we got back to my house the children were so tuckered out they were fast asleep so I told my son to get the pies off the counter and I would see him sometime tomorrow sometime. Just like his brother, he loved "sweet potato pies". This made his day! I also knew that he was "greedy" when it came to these pies he preferred not to share these goodies with nobody.

Now I was still outside getting the children together to put them in his car. He came back out empty handed just when I had finished. I was wondering what was taking him so long. I asked him why he didn't get the pies and he said, "You have to come and see this". So when I go back inside with him I see that there were these fingerprints embedded in both pies. I know for a fact that after I wrapped them when I sat them on the counter earlier there was nothing wrong with them. They were exactly where I left them. Just the two of us had keys to my house.

For some reason I didn't get scared because we both knew that this was exactly what my oldest son used to do. It assured him that nobody else would want to eat the pies except him. He was right! My youngest would get so mad at him. We just stood there staring at the fingerprints for a minute. THEN we both noticed at the same time that there was a slight space between the wrapping and the pie right there in the middle. You could see that wrap itself had not been tampered with. You know the kind you see in the stores. In other words it didn't go through the wrapping. This didn't seem to bother him either nor did it stop him from eating by no means. He was always starving! I personally didn't even want to see any more food. Still I wondered if this was my son's way of telling us that he was still right there on the scene, only in a different form.

Chapter 15

THE GRANDS

Most weekends I would gladly take care of my grandchildren either at my house or theirs while my son and his wife worked. I don't know if you are aware of this or not but children are great psychologist. They watch everything that you do and know just how they can manipulate you. For instance whenever my two would come over with one of their parents they would already have their own agenda laid out. They would literally strip down to their underwear then run over to me in those tiny little voices and ask, "Can we stay with you?" Of course they could, seeing that they had already made themselves at home.

Now my son was having problems with his landlord so they moved in with me while they tried to straighten things out. This was also a good chance to save some money so they could get back on their feet.

One morning after breakfast my youngest son and I were sitting around reminiscing about one thing and another somehow the conversation wound its way around to my oldest son. I had my grandson on my lap when he just blurted out of the blue, "Cashew, Cashew", with this kind of faraway look in his eyes. I just stopped talking while I gathered my thoughts and I asked my son if he had ever told him that was his uncle's nickname. He was stunned too because while he's blurting this out he's pointing to someone or something that we couldn't see. Now he's really to young to remember his uncle and I seriously doubt that he even knew what a cashew nut was.

I get them dressed and later on we went out to feed the ducks in the park that's a couple of miles away. When we get back I notice my grandson felt slightly her feverish after eating lunch. A short time later he vomited all over himself and I thought about this virus that was going around. I gave him a bath and while I was tucking him into my bed he again repeated, "Cashew, Cashew", in almost a whisper only this time it was like he was calling to him and I felt a presence also.

Out of curiosity I asked him, "Do you see him?" He pointed to a corner of the room and said "Over there", and he had this faraway look in his eyes. I left him alone and closed the door so he could get some rest. When he woke up about three hours later the fever was gone and the virus had passed.

Not too long after this, I was awakened one night to the sound of my grand daughter's laughter. She was so loud you would have thought there were more children around. I just had to see what was going one and I couldn't imagine what in the world my son would be doing up at two a.m. knowing that he would have to work the next morning. I thought everybody was asleep so when I peep in the spare room I see her hitting her daddy on the arm trying to wake him up. She's saying, "Daddy wook"! She is clearly trying to show him something. It wasn't until I turned on the light that my son actually did wake up. He didn't have a clue as to what was going one. I took her to the "potty" and put her back to sleep and that's where she stayed until everybody woke up the next morning.

Chapter 16

DENAE

She was so tiny you could literally put her in the palm of you hand. She looked like a beautiful little doll with dimples. My daughter-in-law who is really like my own daughter had complications early on. I cautioned her about having children so fast. "Give your body time to heal up some", I told her before this baby came. My son had to take her to the hospital one night after she passed out so I knew that this time around it be different. As it turned out Denae came at five and one half months.

They now kept her in the intensive care unit with tubes and wires going everywhere. I could have visited her more but I just hated to see her like that. I more or less relied on my son for the updates on how well her progress was coming along. She was a real little fighter according to the specialists. My two grandchildren were really excited especially my granddaughter, she always talked about her baby sister. She was old enough to go visit her and would go with one of her parents at least three times a week. One day she came to tell me how big the baby had gotten.

Now normally I am the first to buy the clothes and cribs for my babies. As a matter of fact, I go out of my way to make sure they have everything they need before they have the first shower. I didn't do that this time because I had a wait and see attitude.

I inquired about her progress after we settled in one night and really didn't like what I heard. I listened intently as my son had nothing but despair in his voice and sounded like he wanted to give up, this was not like him. I tried to give him some kind of hope by saying stuff like "miracles still happen". He didn't want to hear it! The next night there was no change in her condition. I called the hospital but couldn't get any information. I would go after my classes tomorrow to see for myself what's going on. When I laid down later that night I was definitely not settled due to the circumstances, I needed to know. At this point everything was like a big secret but I knew something was wrong.

I dreamt of my oldest son and we are in like a museum together. I have always taken lots of pictures of my children while they were growing up. Here we were looking up at all of his baby pictures even up to the time when he got ill and I was the narrator. Incidentally, whenever I dream about my son we do have conversations however, it is like mental telepathy. I mean we communicate on a different level sort of like I'm reading his mind! Toward the end I remember asking him why he wanted me to see all of his pictures. He looked like he wanted to cry really, with his back to me when he said, "Mama I was sent back here to get Denae"! I wanted to ask him what he meant by that but just like that he was gone. Now this really blew my mind. This was on a Wednesday. It didn't really register until the next day or so.

Thursday I had some classes and rushed out the house so I wouldn't be late. It wasn't until later like in the afternoon that I would recall this dream and spoke about it over lunch with some close friends. They were so scared even one of them said the hairs on her neck stood up so I didn't say anymore about it. I even had to question myself as to, "who am I that the Creator thought enough about me to send my child to tell me that my granddaughter was not going to make it". Shocking but true, I still get a chill just thinking about it! It was like I was forewarned ahead of time. I wanted to tell my son in the worst kind of way but decided against it. I guess I just didn't want him to give up! I didn't want him to be hurt.

That evening when my son and his wife came in I asked them about the baby again. His voice was down to a hush and he spoke gravely about her condition. He was really hurting inside. She was blowing up because of all the medications and the toxins had taken over her little body. She actually looked she was like an overfed nine month old and her vital organs were shutting down.

The next morning, which was Friday I didn't go to any of my classes that's because my son said that he wanted to have a prayer vigil. So when I get to the hospital both sides of the family are there and when I see my granddaughter she is really like a little blimp. Her face is distorted because of all the tubes she had in her little mouth still she was beautiful to me. There was a doctor monitoring the machines and I thought this was not good. As fast as one stopped he would start it up again and they kept drawing blood which I thought was futile. It was now left up to the parents as to what they wanted to do. They decided to pull the plug on Saturday and before they left out of that room you could hear the baby take that last, long deep breath.

When I finally got a chance to hold her in my arms she was dressed and she was leaking so after a few minutes I kissed her softly and put her down. I cried even though I knew that this was best for her and everybody else. If she had survived we would have enormous hospital bills because of all the operations and God only knows what else. My other two grandchildren took the news very well. They are fresh off the press so to speak. They kept on playing when we broke the news to them. They understood why their sister was not coming home. Shortly afterwards we had her cremated. I feel like I now have a little angel and she's now in a better place somewhere on the other side.

Chapter 17

BROTHERS' EXPERIENCES

My youngest brother is still incarcerated and the best way to keep in touch is through letter writing as the phone bills can easily come out looking like a car payment. I brought him up to date on the news. In the meantime he has a court hearing coming up which I regret I couldn't attend due to the circumstances with my mother among other things.

I knew that my other brothers' would be sure to be there for moral support, character witnesses along with a host of friends and other relatives. I kept real close tabs on the upcoming event.

On the day of the sentencing my youngest brother called me. He had to tell me about a strange thing that happened to him. My mind was racing now as he told me how he was sitting down when an entity sat down right beside him. He said, "I felt the bench go down from the weight and then he spoke to me like I'm talking to you right now and said, "You won't get sentenced for "first degree murder" You will get "voluntary manslaughter" instead. He said that he turned to look to his right and left then around the whole room but there was no one there. He said he thought he was going "crazy" because he felt the breath in his ear. When he stood up to speak to the family of the victim he almost fell. The judge then went on to read the sentence and just like the voice said he got the lesser charge of "voluntary manslaughter". I could tell he was really shook up behind this. These are some of the same experiences that I have had all of my life but he didn't believe it until . . . . . it happened to him. To comfort him I told him that he probably wouldn't be incarcerated that long. Secretly, not because he was in this situation, I was glad because now he found out *first hand* what I had been telling him so many times before. He is very practical and if he doesn't see something he just doesn't believe it. He knows otherwise now.

On another occasion I thought it best not to tell him about our oldest brothers' death over the telephone. I wanted to wait until the funeral was over to go see him and tell him myself. On the day I got there, he couldn't wait to tell me about another experience as he asked me about what time our older brother died. I told him around three a.m. I asked why and he stated, "I already knew he had died I was lying on my bunk reading when something that I couldn't see punched me on my arm around the same time". He said, "I figured that it was his way of letting him know that he had checked out". You should have seen his eyes he was really bewildered! When I spoke to my other brothers' they said they didn't tell him because they had to go through too many changes whenever they called the prison they were just going to give him an obituary and explain when they went to see about him. Unlike him I didn't laugh because I understood firsthand what he had experienced. As of this writing my brother has been released.

www.ingramcontent.com/pod-product-compliance
Lightning Source LLC
Chambersburg PA
CBHW020407290526
45785CB00005B/2463